# Who helps us?

# In a hospital

Vic Parker

Heinemann
LIBRARY

Little Nippers

**www.heinemann.co.uk/library**
Visit our website to find out more information about **Heinemann Library** books.

To order:
☎ Phone 44 (0) 1865 888066
▤ Send a fax to 44 (0) 1865 314091
▭ Visit the Heinemann Bookshop at www.heinemann.co.uk/library to browse our catalogue and order online.

First published in Great Britain by Heinemann Library, Halley Court, Jordan Hill, Oxford OX2 8EJ, part of Harcourt Education. Heinemann is a registered trademark of Harcourt Education Ltd.

Editorial: Jilly Attwood and Claire Throp
Design: Jo Hinton-Malivoire and bigtop, Bicester, UK
Models made by: Jo Brooker
Picture Research: Rosie Garai
Production: Séverine Ribierre

Originated by Dot Gradations
Printed and bound in China by South China Printing Company

ISBN 0 431 17320 6 (hardback)
08 07 06 05 04
10 9 8 7 6 5 4 3 2 1

ISBN 0 431 17325 7  (paperback)
08 07 06 05 04
10 9 8 7 6 5 4 3 2 1

**British Library Cataloguing in Publication Data**
Parker, Vic
In a hospital – (Who helps us?)
610.6'9
A full catalogue record for this book is available from the British Library.

**Acknowledgements**
The publishers would like to thank the following for permission to reproduce photographs: Custom Medical Stock Photo pp. **8**, **23**; Peter Evans Photography pp. **4**, **5**, **6**, **7**, **9**, **11**, **12–13**, **14–15**, **16**, **17**, **18**, **19**, **20–21**, **22**; Sally and Richard Greenhill p. **10**.

Cover photograph reproduced with permission of Peter Evans Photography.

The publishers would like to thank Annie Davy for her assistance in the preparation of this book.

Every effort has been made to contact copyright holders of any material reproduced in this book. Any omissions will be rectified in subsequent printings if notice is given to the publishers.

**2**

# Contents

# Into a hospital

Hospitals are busy places.

5

# Visiting a ward

# Having an operation

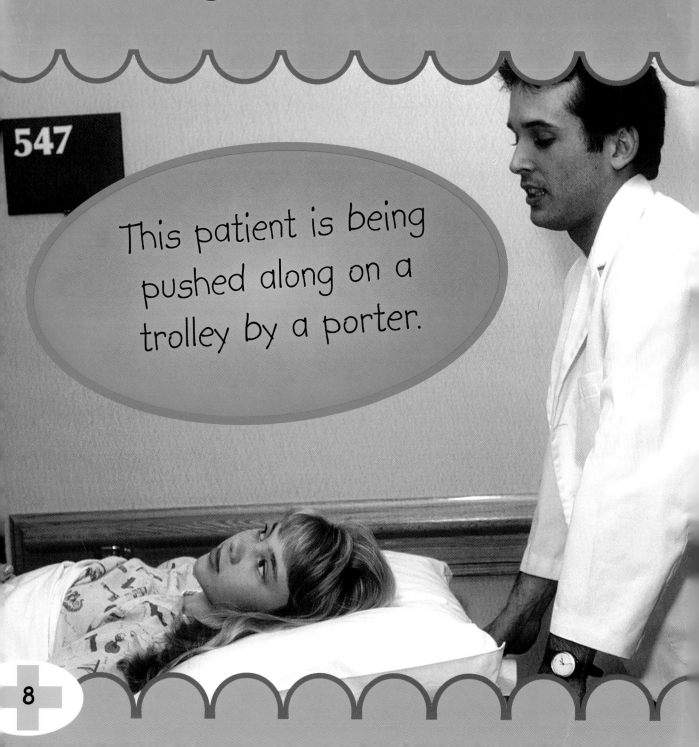

This patient is being pushed along on a trolley by a porter.

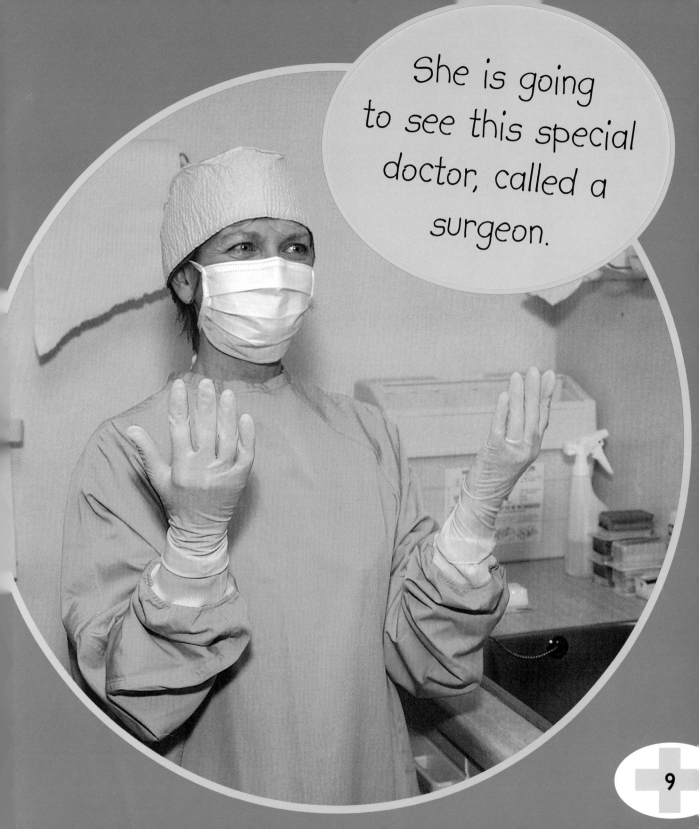

# Staying in hospital

## Some hospitals have a school.

teacher

Some hospitals have a radio station too.

This DJ is playing music for everyone.

# It's an emergency!

**Ne-nah! Ne-nah!**

Here comes an ambulance crew with another patient.

EMERGENCY AMBULANCE

12

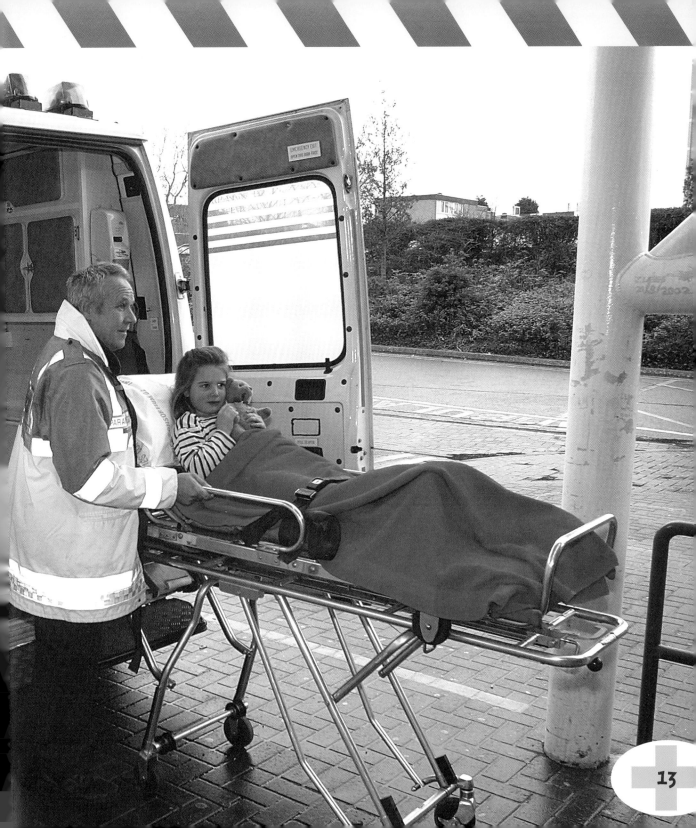

13

The doctor will soon find out by doing special tests.

# A special machine

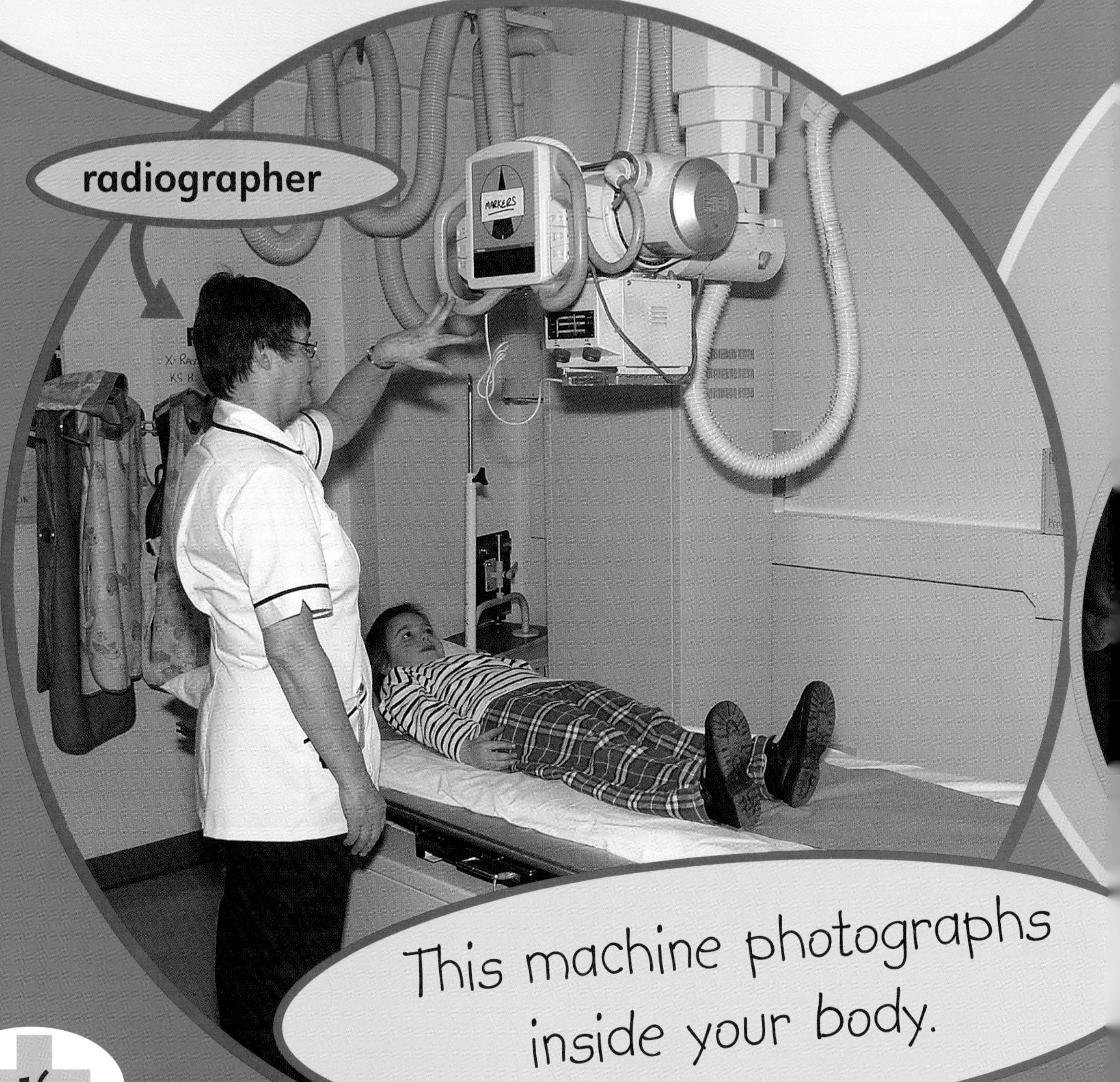

radiographer

This machine photographs inside your body.

16

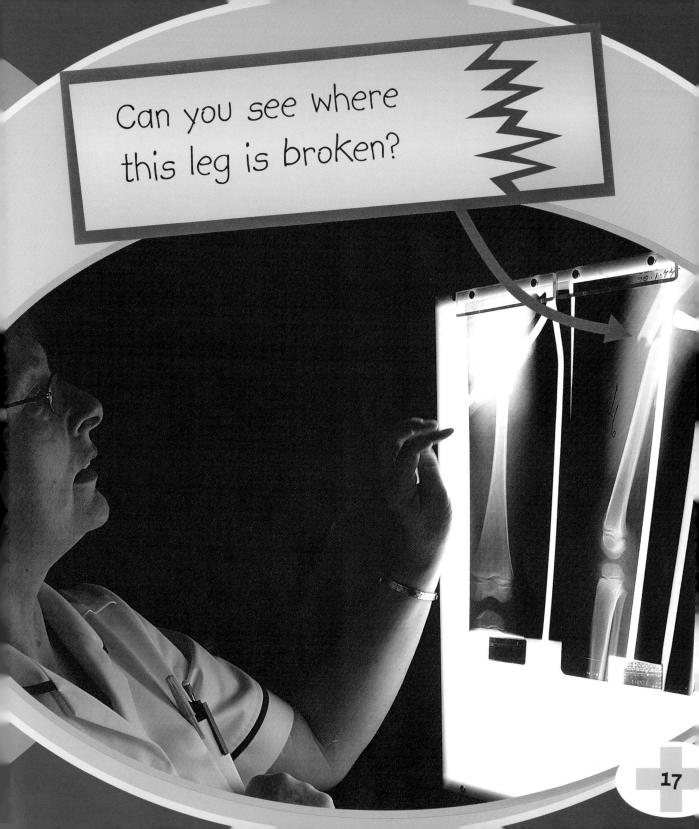

Can you see where this leg is broken?

# There, there!

This **wet** plaster will soon go hard and **stiff**.

It will keep the broken bone **straight** while it mends.

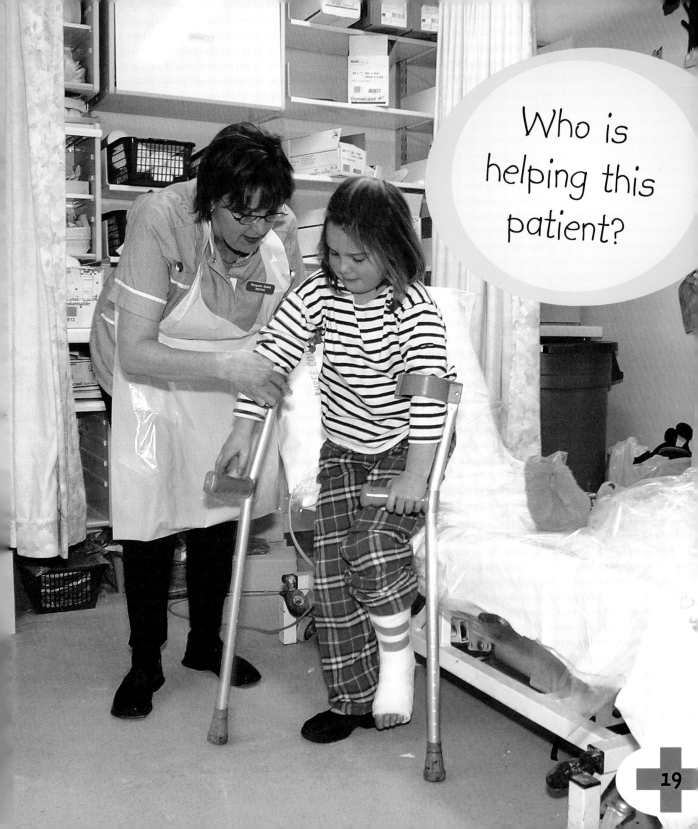

Who is helping this patient?

# Picking up medicine

pharmacist

In a hospital, there are lots of different medicines to make you well.

# Feeling better

Some people need special exercises to make them better.

physiotherapist

This hospital helper is hard at work too.

Can you guess who it is?

# Index

The end

## Notes for adults

The *Who helps us . . .?* series looks at a variety of people that a young child may come across in different situations. The books explore who these people are, why we might interact with them, and how to communicate appropriately. Used together, the books will enable discussion about similarities and differences between environments and people, and encourage the growth of the child's sense of self. The following Early Learning Goals are relevant to this series:

*Knowledge and understanding of the world*
Early learning goals for a sense of place:
• show an interest in the world in which they live
• notice differences between features of the local environment
• observe, find out about and identify features in the place they live and the natural world
• find out about their environment, and talk about those features they like and dislike.

*Personal, social and emotional development*
Early learning goals for a sense of community:
• make connections between different parts of their life experience
• understand that people have different needs, views, cultures and beliefs, which need to be treated with respect.
Early learning goals for self-confidence and self-esteem:
• separate from main carer with support/confidence
• express needs and feelings in appropriate ways

• initiate interactions with other people
• have a sense of self as a member of different communities
• respond to significant experiences, showing a range of feelings when appropriate
• have a developing awareness of their own needs, views and feelings and be sensitive to the needs, views and feelings of others.

This book introduces the reader to a range of people they may come across when at a hospital. It will encourage young children to think about the jobs these people perform and how they help the community. **In a hospital** will help children extend their vocabulary, as they will hear new words such as *operation* and *pharmacist*. You may like to introduce and explain other new words yourself, such as *stretcher* and *x-ray*.

**Follow-up activities**
• Use a toy doctor's kit to explain and role play routine procedures such as taking a temperature, using a stethoscope, putting on a bandage etc.
• Explain the difference between tablets and sweeties, and that only grown-ups should touch medicines. The child could draw a picture of a doctor or a nurse giving a patient some medicine to make them better.
• Make a toys' hospital with a cardboard cut-out ambulance, shoe box beds and scraps of material for bandages.